30 DAYS
TO VICTORY
THROUGH
FORGIVENESS

T O N Y   E V A N S

HARVEST HOUSE PUBLISHERS
EUGENE, OREGON

Cover by Dugan Design Group, Bloomington, Minnesota

Cover photo © Terry Dugan

30 DAYS TO VICTORY THROUGH FORGIVENESS
Copyright © 2015 Tony Evans
Published by Harvest House Publishers
Eugene, Oregon 97402
www.harvesthousepublishers.com

ISBN 978-0-7369-6185-1 (pbk.)
ISBN 978-0-7369-6186-8 (eBook)

Printed in the United States of America

15 16 17 18 19 20 21 22 23 / BP-JH / 10 9 8 7 6 5 4 3 2 1

CONTENTS

INTRODUCTION

A few years ago, I came down with the flu. I rarely get sick, but this lasted for a week. On Sunday morning, I stumbled to my closet, threw on some clothes, and made it as far as the garage.

My wife, Lois, saw me sitting in the car looking flushed and weak, and she said, "Tony, please stay home just this once." In nearly four decades of being a pastor, I had never missed a Sunday because of illness. But this time, she was right. I was in no position to drive to the church, let alone deliver two hour-long sermons.

The flu that gripped my body that week and knocked me to my knees illustrates what unforgiveness can do in your life. It can control your choices and actions.

Carrying the burden of yesterday can drain you of your energy until you can't live out the life God has in store for you. It's like lugging around your belongings in several backpacks and bags when traveling instead of pulling them easily in a suitcase on wheels. The number of items you are carrying may be the same, but how you choose to carry them determines how tired you feel, how fast you walk, and how easily you can go up or down stairs. If you accumulate too many of these overstuffed backpacks, you become immobilized.

If this sounds like your life, be encouraged because God sees you worn-out and stumbling where you should be running. He sees you throwing stuff together instead of fully expressing your gifts and skills. He sees you lugging around more than you were ever designed to. If you will only rest in Him, He will show you the way to move through life more effortlessly.

I didn't preach that Sunday I was sick. Instead, I listened to my wife's advice. I got out of the car, went back to bed, and immediately fell asleep. The next week, I ate the healthy food she prepared for me and did what my doctor said to do. As a result, I got better. By the next Sunday, I was back in the pulpit again.

God has a plan for your life and energy too. It may take time and will surely require discipline. You need to rest in Him. You also need to eat the healthy food He has prepared for you, such as wisdom from His Word and times of intimacy with Him. If you will listen to Him and do what He says, He will restore you and give you strength to live the way He designed you to.

In 40 years of counseling people living in defeat, I've

found that unforgiveness has been the most common problem. We all need to forgive at some point. Unforgiveness affects everyone, often keeping people from fulfilling God's plan for their lives. That's why I'm so passionate about sharing these principles with you over the course of the next month. It's time to be free.

RESULTS OF UNFORGIVENESS

DAY ONE

The story is told about two monks who were traveling together and had to cross a river. An elderly, heavyset woman was seated at the bank of the river, waiting for someone to help her across.

The river was wide, so the monks decided to take turns carrying the woman across. One monk hoisted her onto his back and carried her halfway across, and the other monk carried her the rest of the way. The woman thanked them for their generous help, and they bid her farewell.

As the monks continued their walk, the first monk began to complain of pain in his back. The second monk assured him it was nothing. But before long the first monk began to complain again and had to stop to rest.

The second monk asked, "Why are we stopping?"

"It's my back," the first monk said. "It hurts from carrying that woman. Doesn't yours?"

"No," the second monk replied, "I set her down two miles ago."

The first monk was still weighed down by the woman even though she was long gone. He was still feeling the effects of having her on his back. By continuing to think about what he had carried, he was unable to continue on his way and reach his destination.

Unforgiveness sits like a burden on your back. Even though the offense may be long gone, it can continue to weigh you down, keeping you from your destination. You can become immobilized by being caught up in the pain of the past. Yesterday's burdens can weigh you down today and prevent you from reaching a brighter tomorrow.

I'm sure this comes as no surprise. Painful experiences in your past can easily burden your heart, mind, soul, and body today. These hurts could be from your distant childhood or from last week.

Having counseled hundreds of people, I've seen a repeated pattern of pain cropping up from the past. Most often, the pain is from someone's childhood or young adult years. Time has moved on, but healing hasn't progressed at the same pace. The memories and the impact are difficult to shake.

Some folks say that time heals all wounds, but I disagree. I've seen too many people carry too many wounds for too long. On the other hand, I've seen other people heal from deep wounds in a relatively short time. Time doesn't heal all wounds—but God can. When you align your perspective with His perspective on pain, you can experience healing too. The first step to victory through forgiveness is to realize that God always has a purpose for your pain. Therefore, you don't need to carry the burdens of the past. You can let them go.

DAY TWO

The *Pelicano* was once the most unwelcome ship in the world. For more than two years it sailed the open seas—the *Flying Dutchman* of the twentieth century.

The massive ship was turned away from ports in Honduras, Costa Rica, Guinea-Bissau, Cape Verde, the Bahamas, and many more. It wandered the Caribbean, crossed the Atlantic to West Africa, sailed the Mediterranean, and roamed the Indian Ocean. It was allowed to dock only long enough to refuel. During those years, the *Pelicano* changed names twice and owners once.

The widespread rejection of the *Pelicano* began in 1986 when sanitation workers in Philadelphia went on strike for almost a month. As trash accumulated, the city tried to ship it to Ohio and Georgia, but those states said no deal. Philadelphia eventually incinerated the

trash and dumped 28 million pounds of scrap and ash—
including toxic elements, such as arsenic and lead—into
the belly of a ship later named the *Pelicano*.

No port in the world wanted anything to do with it.

I didn't experience the strike in Philadelphia first-
hand, but I did experience a similar situation when my
wife and I took a trip to Venice. Throughout the city,
we saw (and smelled) mounds of trash. The streets were
already narrow, but now they were littered with trash
heaps as well. The odor made alleys unbearable.

When we asked what had happened, we learned that
sanitation workers were on strike in Venice.

Needless to say, I have very few fond memories of
that trip. The stench of other people's debris caused
everyone to suffer, including us. The beauty of the city's
exquisite architecture and the tranquility of a gondola
ride on a canal are difficult to enjoy when you are hit by
such a horrible smell.

Unforgiveness can do that in your life as well. When
left unattended and allowed to pile up, it begins to affect
everything you do and everyone around you. The fresh,
clean atmosphere of love for God and for other people
becomes polluted by unforgiveness. Kind words become
biting. Giving gestures are tied to expectations and
demands. Sweetness is laced with bitterness.

In other words, you can no longer be the loving person God created you to be. Instead, the debris of rotting

regret, shame, and anger poison the air, causing difficulties in your relationships, your career, and other areas of your life. That's why forgiveness is so important. It restores the person who hurt you, it frees you from regret, and it empowers you to regain the life you were meant to have.

DAY THREE

Life sometimes has a way of unloading its junk on us, doesn't it? We might feel as if we are like the *Pelicano*, burdened with the toxic waste of poor choices (others' or our own).

The overpowering fumes of anger, guilt, pessimism, fear, and bitterness drive other people away from us, and we drift along aimlessly, just as the *Pelicano* did. We jump in and out of relationships, situations, jobs...only to discover that we are welcome long enough to take on a little fuel but no longer. No one wants our trash.

Living this way will make you weary, and weariness dictates how you will feel and what you will do. When you are weary, you can't relax. You can't feel at home with who you are. You lose your peace. You are no longer trusting, free, caring, and giving.

But as you begin experiencing victory through

forgiveness, you rediscover the beauty of being the person God created you to be. You see God turning your mess into a miracle. You realize He is transforming your tragedy into triumph, your burden into a blessing.

This is similar to what eventually happened with the *Pelicano*. No one knows exactly where the ship is today, but the story is that it was eventually retired.

Like most ships of its size, once it had served its time, it is believed to have been recycled into scrap metal. Pieces of its hull might be found in a car carrying a happy family around India today. Fragments of its deck might make up the shell of a tractor plowing a field of corn in Ohio. Portions of its bow might be in a schoolchild's desk in New Jersey or in the playground equipment in the schoolyard. And sections of its bulwark might be part of a bridge over a bay.

Wherever the *Pelicano* is, it no longer carries its weight. And because of that, it was set free to become more than anyone ever imagined it would.

It has become a blessing and no longer a burden.

God wants you to be a blessing too—to those around you, to Him, and to yourself. But that can happen only when you take the steps necessary to truly forgive.

DAY FOUR

If Satan can convince you to focus on your past, he can keep you from fulfilling all you were created to be. Yet God invites you to look at your future (Jeremiah 29:11). The enemy says, "You can't—because of the damage that has been done!" But God says, "You can—in spite of what has been done!" The enemy will define you by your past in order to confine you. But God will set you free, showing you who you really are by pointing you toward your future

Friend, never let your yesterday keep you from your tomorrow. Learn from yesterday but don't live in it.

The Israelites struggled with this after escaping 430 years of domination in Egypt. The Israelites had left Egypt, but Egypt had not left them. As they sent spies into the Promised Land, they stood on the precipice of a glorious tomorrow. But they chose to focus on yesterday's sorrows rather than tomorrow's challenges, so they did not move forward. They looked at life through the rear-view mirror rather than the windshield of opportunity.

God had delivered the Israelites *from* their past (Egypt) and *to* their future (Canaan). Yet they chose to focus on yesterday, so they missed the opportunity. As a result, they wandered in the wilderness for 40 years— long enough for God to disconnect them from their past.

For many of us, tomorrow never comes because we

are tied to our past. We're carrying so much baggage from yesterday, we can't even get through today, let alone step into our future. You may have suffered an offense long ago, but if you are still struggling to forgive, it is still holding you back today.

The Israelites were tethered to their past because they failed to let go and move on. They could have walked from Egypt to Canaan in 35 days. But the trip lasted 40 years because they kept looking back.

Does that sound familiar to you? Do you feel as if you should have been further in your life by now—further in your career, your relationships, your family, your finances, or your emotional and spiritual well-being? If so, notice where you're looking. Is it in the rearview mirror or through the windshield?

How can you tell? Here's one way. Do you often think, *What if…?* or *Why…?* or *If only…?*

You might fear that because of what happened to you, you will never regain the hope you once knew. You may fear that someone has messed you up too much, stolen your innocence, or ruined your future.

Yesterday is real—there's no denying it. But make sure you're not looking at it so much that you miss out on today and thus dim the light of your tomorrow.

When someone sins against you or you commit sins you regret, your soul is wounded. If that wound is left untreated, the sore will fester and the pain will increase.

If someone accidentally brushes up against your wound, you'll jolt in pain and lash out at them.

To experience victory through forgiveness, make sure to treat your wounds. Let them heal, and rather than focusing on the scars of your past, focus on your new start. It's a new day. Live in it. Take it one step at a time. One moment at a time. Live in forgiveness today, not the pain of yesterday, and step by step, you will move into a victorious tomorrow.

DAY FIVE

How do you climb a mountain? One step at a time. Forgiveness is a lot like that as well. It's a long process with small victories along the way. You may feel as if you have forgiven someone or yourself, only to have something trigger those same raw emotions of anger, bitterness, fear, and regret. I want to encourage you—if that happens, don't give up. Keep climbing, step by step. Eventually you'll get there. It's a process.

But there are some mountains that God doesn't want you to climb. He wants you to move them.

Maybe you're facing an impossible situation in your life right now—a circumstance that seems to be insurmountable. You can't fix it or change it, and regardless of how hard you look, you can't see any light at the end of the tunnel. You can't climb over this mountain. You can't dig through it. You feel stuck at the base of it.

Your insurmountable situation may be professional or relational. It could have to do with your health or a personal vice you are trying to overcome. Whatever it is, it seems too high, too wide, too thick, and too steep to overcome. The Bible uses a mountain like this as a picture of a situation you cannot solve, a struggle you cannot win, or a pain you cannot dull (Zechariah 4:7).

When Jesus taught us how to pray, He said that faith the size of a mustard seed could move a mountain (Mark 11:22-24). Then He gave us a clue as to why our prayers may not be moving much of anything at all. In the next few verses of Mark 11, we read, "Whenever you stand praying, forgive, if you have anything against anyone, so that your Father who is in heaven will also forgive you your transgressions. [But if you do not forgive, neither will your Father who is in heaven forgive your transgressions.]"

If you have not yet overcome the mountain you are facing in your life right now, forgiveness may be the key to victory.

Before God can empower you to move the mountains you are facing, you must forgive. Moving mountains is conditioned on the purity of your relationship with God. And the purity of that relationship usually hinges on forgiveness. If anything blocks the flow of God's power in your life more than all else, it is unforgiveness.

Here is the point I want you to focus on today: You have a mountain in your life that you want God to supernaturally move. And He will, but there's a condition. Jesus tells us that you must forgive other people in order to experience relational forgiveness with God.

Keep in mind, this is not speaking in terms of legal forgiveness—or salvation, which Christ secured on the cross. Just as you can be legally married but relationally miserable, you can experience legal forgiveness (salvation) without experiencing relational forgiveness (closeness with God).

Here's how this works. When you offer forgiveness to others, God offers His relational forgiveness to you. When you experience that closeness with God, the channel is open for Him to hear and answer your prayers—including your prayers for Him to move the mountain in your life.

So faith that forgives is faith that moves mountains. It's believing that God is sovereign and that He uses painful experiences for your good. When you don't forgive someone, you reveal that you don't believe God had a purpose for that pain.

"Forgiveness" is a beautiful word when someone is giving it to you. But it's not such a beautiful word when you have to give it to someone else. God has given us much more forgiveness than we will ever have to give. So if we are not able to forgive others, there is evidently a breach in our fellowship and intimacy with Him. Conversely, as we meditate on the incredible forgiveness He has given us, we will have a deep well of forgiveness to share with others.

"Forgive us our debts, as we also have forgiven our debtors" (Matthew 6:12).

To receive relational forgiveness from God—and the faith to move mountains—learn to forgive.

DAY SIX

What are some of the things that are necessary if we are to experience victory through forgiveness? We've looked at a few already this week.

- Recognize the damage you can cause by carrying around your pain. Unforgiveness dampens your joy, slows you down, creates distance between you and God, and keeps you from entering His destiny for your life.

- Acknowledge your pain. It's real and raw to you, and it deserves to be addressed.

- Remember that unforgiveness affects those

around you even if you don't intend it to. Your festering wounds fill the atmosphere around you with the stench of unforgiveness.

- Notice the way forgiveness helps you keep all your relationships healthy. It frees you to overlook small offenses and share your love and generosity.

- Don't let the weight of yesterday ruin today and tomorrow.

When someone wounds you and you choose to not forgive them, you lock them up inside a prison within your own heart. The problem is, you also join them there. In order to let yourself out of the confinement of bitterness and resentment, you need to let them out as well.

Tomorrow's reading is titled "Prayers and Practicals." It includes a prayer to guide you through what we've learned this week. Take time to write down your own prayers too. Talk with God about what you've learned or how you feel about what happened to you that you need to forgive.

After the prayer, I've listed a few practical steps you can take this week on your journey to victory through forgiveness.

Starting next week, we are going to look at three kinds of forgiveness: unilateral, transactional, and personal. Each one is important in its own way.

DAY SEVEN

Prayers and Practicals

*Dear Father, I've carried around this weight
of unforgiveness far too long. It's burdened
my soul and sapped me of the strength and
joy You have made me to experience. I've lost
hours and days to bitterness, coping, and
rehearsing the events of my past in my head. I
don't want to live this way anymore. I know
that it's creating distance in my relationship
with You, and it's also causing friction in my
relationships. Please join me on this journey of
release. Open my mind and heart to understand
Your truth. Give me the willingness to apply
the principles and the power to forgive.*

Prayer Needs and Requests

_____

_____

_____

_____

_____

_____

My Own Prayer

_____

_____

_____

_____

_____

_____

Practicals

1. Write down several relationships or areas in your life in which you need to forgive. How has unforgiveness affected the way you relate to others or the way you choose to cope?

2. List two of your dreams or ambitions—even if you have given up on them. Experiencing them now might seem as impossible as moving a mountain. Write them down anyway and remember them as you walk through this process of forgiveness. These are your goals. Victory through forgiveness can help you reach them.

3. Choose one person you need to forgive. Every day this next week, pray a simple prayer that God will bless this person. Feel free to add more people to this list if you want.

WEEK TWO

TYPES OF FORGIVENESS

DAY ONE

Some time ago, Lois and I took a highly anticipated trip to Hawaii. It followed several months of a heavy work schedule, so we were really looking forward to some peace and quiet and rest. We couldn't wait to see the refreshing views and hear the calming sounds of the sea. I was scheduled to preach at a conference in Hawaii, so we maximized the opportunity by tagging on a few vacation days afterward. We needed it. When we boarded our flight, we were tired and worn-out. But we knew that once we got there, all would be well.

We were wrong.

A few minutes after unpacking our bags, we discovered that the resort hotel where we were staying was undergoing a major renovation. No one had bothered to let us know. Hammers pounded and power saws screeched nonstop from early morning until late each evening. Needless to say, the noise drowned out the sounds of the ocean waves and distracted us from what we had come there to do—rest and recoup so we could move forward with strength.

To top it off, toward the end of this already chaotic trip, I became so sick that I had to be rushed to the hospital. I had never experienced that level of pain before. Doubling over in the car on the frantic drive to the hospital, I thought, *This isn't how Hawaii is supposed to be.* It was awful. I had to stay in the hospital a couple days, but at least I was away from the noisy hotel!

By the time Lois and I boarded the plane back to Dallas, we were worse off than when we had left.

Isn't it amazing what someone else's mess will do to you? It can keep you from enjoying the beauty around you and from getting what you need in order to be strong. It's also amazing what problems your own mess can cause.

Whether it's your own or someone else's, a mess distracts you, blocks your view, and slows down your progress. Like a crying baby on an airplane, it saps the energy and attention you intended to direct elsewhere.

Sin is essentially mess. Whether you need to forgive someone who has sinned against you or forgive yourself for your own sin that is causing guilt and shame, it's mess. And mess has a way of preventing you from being all that you were created to be.

That's why forgiveness is so important. When you forgive, you free yourself from the mess around you and in you.

DAY TWO

Before we can look at the different types of forgiveness, we need to clarify what forgiveness is. This is important because many people simply don't know what forgiveness is or whether they have forgiven, and that confusion causes problems. I have counseled plenty of people who say they have forgiven, but their words and actions tell another story.

To experience victory through forgiveness, we must define and live it out correctly. Biblical forgiveness is the decision to...

- not seek vengeance against an offender
- release the offender from all debt
- cancel the blame the offender deserves

Keep in mind that forgiveness is a decision first, not an emotion. It's not about how you feel but rather about your choice to no longer credit an offense or blame against an offender (even if that offender is yourself).

The best biblical basis for this definition of forgiveness is in 1 Corinthians 13:5, where we discover that love "keeps no record of wrongs" (NIV). That doesn't mean love justifies the wrong (enabling), ignores it (denying), excuses it (rationalizing), or pretends it didn't happen (lying). Like an alcoholic's spouse continuing to clean up the mess from the previous night's disaster, these inappropriate responses only close the door to healing and open the door for the offense (the sin) to continue. That's not love.

Love means not keeping a record of the wrong. This is how God forgives us. He doesn't forget the sin, but He no longer holds the offense against our account. We are not in debt to Him, required to pay off something that we are unable to pay.

This doesn't always mean you will relate to the person the same way you did before the offense. But it does mean that you no longer hold it against them. This keeps your heart free from the dangerous emotions of anger, revenge, guilt, or shame. Instead, you love them. Even if reconciliation isn't possible, you can love the person by speaking of them appropriately and taking them before the Lord in prayer.

What do you need to forgive? Is it someone else's mess that spilled over into your life (like the renovation project at the hotel), or is it your own mess (like the illness that landed me in the hospital)? Either way, leave the mess behind by offering forgiveness, and you will be free to pursue your destiny. It's time to forgive.

DAY THREE

A little bird was flying south for the winter, but the air became so cold that it began to freeze and could not continue the trip to a warmer climate. The little bird finally collapsed in a large field where a herd of cows stood grazing. Eventually, a cow came by and dropped manure on the freezing bird. At first, the bird was very upset, but then it realized how warm the manure felt. Before too long, the small bird thawed out and became so excited that it started to sing with joy.

Just as it started singing, a cat happened to be passing nearby and heard the bird's happy tune. The cat followed the sounds to the manure pile, discovered the little bird, and ate it.

We can learn three lessons from this tale. First, not everyone who drops manure on you is your enemy. Second, not everyone who digs you out is your friend. Finally, when you're in manure, it's best to keep your mouth shut.

Forgiveness is often a mixed bag. Rarely is it clear-cut. We don't usually know exactly who played what part, to what degree, and how much we have contributed to the situation.

Sometimes people hurt you without meaning to. Sometimes they don't even know they did! These are usually misunderstandings or clashes of values or even worldviews.

Sometimes you think someone is helping you (like the cat digging out the bird), only to find out they actually weren't. These are times of betrayal. You trusted someone, and they tricked you somehow, revealing an ulterior motive. You may even feel as if God has betrayed you, contradicting His Word, which says He loves you and cares for you. When you compare that with the pain in your life, you're confused.

Sometimes we speak when we shouldn't. We speak prematurely, we are impulsive, we react rashly, we jump to conclusions…for whatever reason, we just make the matter worse (like the little bird). Or we gossip and slander those who hurt us, creating even more strife and confusion.

We can interpret the events in our lives in various ways and choose from a broad range of responses. In order to experience victory through forgiveness, we need to understand three different kinds of forgiveness so we can apply the right approach to the right situation. The three kinds of forgiveness are personal, unilateral, and transactional.

DAY FOUR

You may be surprised to discover that we will begin by talking about *personal forgiveness*, or forgiving yourself. Actually, personal *un*forgiveness (resulting in guilt and shame) is one of the most prevalent forms of unforgiveness I see in the people I counsel. Shame and guilt can derail you from pursuing God's purpose for your life far easier than anything else. This is because shame and guilt often lead to coping mechanisms, which in turn lead to even more personal unforgiveness. The downward spiral deepens over time.

Personal unforgiveness also robs you of the confidence and boldness that the Christian life of faith requires. Our Lord often moves in response to our prayers and faith in Him. If you are bound by guilt and shame, you will not approach His throne boldly to ask for wisdom, guidance, and blessing even though He invites you to (Hebrews 4:16). Instead, you will shrink back, assuming that God must be disappointed and upset with you. And if that's the case, you ask yourself, why would He want to hear from you?

The apostle Paul provides a wonderful example of personal forgiveness. If anyone should have held himself back from seeking God's best for his life, Paul should have. After all, Paul used to kill Christians for sport. We read, "I thank Christ Jesus our Lord, who has strengthened me, because He considered me faithful, putting me into service, even though I was formerly a *blasphemer* and a *persecutor* and a *violent aggressor*" (1 Timothy 1:12-13).

You name it, and Paul had done it. In fact, Paul said he was the worst of the worst. "It is a trustworthy statement, deserving full acceptance, that Christ Jesus came into the world to save sinners, *among whom I am foremost* of all. Yet for this reason I found mercy, so that in me as the foremost, *Jesus Christ might demonstrate His perfect patience* as an example for those who would believe in Him" (verses 15-16). Paul is an example to all of us.

In other words, if Christ can forgive Paul, love him, and use him in an extraordinary way for His kingdom and the good of others, He can do the same with anyone. No pit is too deep, no sin too severe, and no thought too wretched to keep anyone from the abundant grace, faith, and love that are in Christ Jesus (verse 14).

Friend, Jesus died for you on the cross in order to forgive you. He took your punishment so that you can live freely in His pardon. To not forgive yourself is to crucify Christ again and again. It is to insult His sacrifice by saying it wasn't good enough. To that I have just one question. If Christ's death was good enough for God to forgive you, isn't it good enough for you to forgive yourself?

If you struggle in this area of personal unforgiveness, then one of your greatest acts of faith just might be to get down on your knees and ask the Lord to bless you. You may not believe you deserve His mercy, grace, and blessing (who does?). But He longs to give them to you. He died to give them to you. Would you take a moment right now to bow before Him and ask Him to bless you—to give you wisdom, grace, love, and the freedom of knowing that nothing you have ever done can separate you from His goodness and care?

Don't try to cover up your past regrets by making new ones. Rather, confess, let it go, and move on into the abundant grace and victory God has for you.

DAY FIVE

When you forgive someone who hasn't asked for forgiveness and may not have even repented of their offense, you are offering *unilateral forgiveness*. You are granting them forgiveness on your own—unilaterally, or without their involvement.

Why would you grant forgiveness to someone who hasn't asked for it and probably doesn't deserve it? Here's the main reason: You do it not to set them free but to set yourself free. You do it so you can keep going. Unilateral forgiveness releases you from something that the other person may never get right. This is what God did on the cross by not "counting their trespasses against them" (2 Corinthians 5:19).

There are other reasons for offering forgiveness unilaterally. The offense might be so small that it's not worth addressing with the other person. Or maybe the offender has died or can't be contacted. Or perhaps the offender simply won't repent, apologize, or even acknowledge what they have done.

In situations like these, if you are unable to unilaterally forgive, you are the one who is held hostage, not the offender. It has been said that refusing to forgive is like drinking poison and expecting someone else to die from it. But of course, you are only poisoning yourself. The bitterness, regret, and anger churning inside you poison your thoughts, override your emotions, distract you from living out your destiny, and jeopardize your relationships.

You cannot change what happened to you, nor can you change the person who did it. You can only change yourself and your response to the offense, so that is where you need to focus.

One day while I was driving, another driver ran into my car—and then sped off! My car was pretty banged up. It was a minor thing in the big scheme of life, but it was a real challenge to me. Every time I looked at my banged-up car, I felt frustration, helplessness, and loss—emotions that often challenge victims of hit-and-run accidents. I dreaded the inconvenience of getting my car fixed and paying the expense, but eventually I had to.

I hadn't done anything to deserve the damage, and the other driver was long gone. But if I left my car banged up, I would always be reminded of what happened that day. I had to fix the car in order to put the situation behind me and move on.

The person who damaged it didn't tell me they were sorry. They didn't offer me their license number or insurance card. They didn't even stop to see if I was okay or if I had been hurt and needed help. But this wasn't about the offender—it was about my ability to live an emotionally healthy life.

Unilateral forgiveness doesn't just release the other person—unilateral forgiveness releases you.

As Stephen, the first martyr of the church, was being stoned to death, he offered unilateral forgiveness. He asked God to forgive those who were killing him. He prayed, "Lord, do not hold this sin against them" (Acts 7:60 NIV).

How could Stephen muster the emotional strength to do this? Verse 56 tells us that he had seen Christ standing at the right hand of God. His clear view of a brighter future and a greater purpose empowered him to forgive those who didn't want or deserve to be forgiven.

Jesus did the same thing on a much larger scale as He hung on the cross. In fact, He died to provide forgiveness for us and to give us the basis of providing forgiveness for others (Ephesians 4:32; Colossians 3:13). When we focus on what Christ did for us on the cross, we find strength to forgive others.

Friend, your offenders may never admit what they did was wrong, let alone say they are sorry. Facing that fact is key if you are to move on. Granting unilateral forgiveness in those situations will keep you from poisoning yourself with bitterness and resentment.

God has a purpose for your pain. Nothing gets to you that does not first pass through His hand. And if He allows it to pass through His hand, He can use it for a greater good if you will but trust Him, seek Him, and see Him, as Stephen did, standing at the right hand of God, exalted above all rulers, powers, and authorities. Don't let other people's offenses or your own pain cloud your view of a brighter tomorrow and your greater purpose.

DAY SIX

We've learned about forgiving ourselves (personal forgiveness) and forgiving those who haven't said "I'm sorry" (unilateral forgiveness). Now let's consider what to do when the offender has repented and sought out your forgiveness. This is the time to offer what we call *transactional forgiveness.* The offender offers an apology, and you offer forgiveness. An exchange takes place—it's a two-way agreement.

Transactional forgiveness restores something that has been broken. People who willingly confess and repent *usually* want the relationship to be reconciled. But here's the trick—we don't always know the real motive behind the offender's confession and repentance. The motivation may be pure, and the person could be truly repentant. But then again, perhaps the offender simply got caught and is trying to avoid the consequences.

Let's briefly review what repentance is. Repentance involves not only being sorry but also having a "change of mind" about the offense—seeing the offense the way God sees it. This then prompts a turning away from the wrong behavior and toward right behavior. It may include an offering of restitution if possible or necessary. The purpose of repentance is not only to reestablish fellowship with God and reconciliation with others but also to limit the consequences of the offense.

Unfortunately, offenders may seem repentant but not really have a "change of mind" about the offense, and so the offense occurs again and again. When this happens, people may continue to say "I'm sorry" but only because they got caught and are trying to avoid the consequences of their actions.

This being so, it's important to note that transactional

forgiveness includes two components—forgiveness and reconciliation. Forgiveness should be granted as soon as possible, but reconciliation should be earned through a demonstration of true repentance and trustworthiness.

So after we offer transactional forgiveness but before we enter into reconciliation, we should test the fruit of repentance. This is what Joseph did when his brothers asked him to forgive them in Egypt. In Genesis 42:15-16, Joseph said he was testing their words—finding out whether they were telling the truth. At that time, his brothers weren't aware he was the brother they had lied about and sold into slavery. But Joseph knew who they were and what they had done to him 22 years earlier. Because of that, he tested their hearts and character to see whether they had changed or had remained the same.

Saying "I'm sorry for what I did" is a good thing. But if that apology is not accompanied by fruits of repentance, it might really mean, "I'm sorry I got caught."

True repentance leads to life. For example, after Peter denied Jesus three times, he went out and wept—and then he returned to serving Christ. On the other hand, Judas merely felt remorse (Matthew 27:3)—and then he went out and hanged himself.

Before you restore a relationship with someone who seeks transactional forgiveness from you, take time to make sure they are offering true repentance and not just remorse. Have they truly turned from the offenses they committed against you?

DAY SEVEN

Prayers and Practicals

Dear Lord, as I continue moving toward victory through forgiveness, I ask that Your Holy Spirit will reveal to me the hurts that are buried deep within me and weighing me down. Show me how I have sinned so I can repent and forgive myself. Uncover sins that others have committed against me so I can experience freedom through forgiveness. Bring these things to my mind and heart and empower me to face them and deal with them as I should.

Prayer Needs and Requests

_____

_____

_____

_____

_____

_____

My Own Prayer

_____

_____

_____

_____

_____

Practicals

1. Do you need to offer anyone unilateral forgiveness? Write down a few names and situations.

2. Has anyone asked you for forgiveness? Write down a name or two and outline some steps you can take toward a process of reconciliation.

3. We once gave our congregation three-by-five cards and asked everyone to write down an offense they needed to forgive. Then we invited them to walk to the front of the church, tear up their card, and place the pieces in trash cans we had put there. You may want to do a similar thing in your home. The process of tearing up the offense symbolizes your willingness to forgive.

4. Do you need to forgive yourself for something? Instead of writing it down, spend a moment right now in prayer, asking for God's heart toward you to be manifest in your heart toward yourself. Ask Him to reveal to you how He sees you—forgiven and not condemned—and enjoy the freedom that comes from forgiving yourself.

WEEK THREE

STEPS TO FORGIVENESS

DAY ONE

As we've been discovering along our 30-day journey, nothing sets you free to arrive at your destiny like forgiveness. Forgiveness is the one thing, above all else, that clears the way for God to move in your life. It releases His hand and opens His heart to take you from where you are to where you are supposed to go. This is because forgiveness aligns your character with His own.

God is holy and dwells in holiness. When you refuse to become bitter about your past, you keep your soul free from the sin of unforgiveness. I'm excited that you're turning from anything that would hold you back and weigh you down—that you're discovering the freedom and future that a life of forgiveness offers you.

For four decades I have offered people counsel from God's Word as they have faced tough things in life— things that just aren't fair. And the pain you've experienced may fall into that category very easily. It might not have been your fault. It might not have been fair. You may have done nothing to deserve it or provoke it.

You served your employer faithfully for 20 years, and when the recession hit, he thanked you with a pink slip. Or you loved and dedicated yourself to your husband and children, and now he has walked out on you for a younger woman. Or your child leapt into adulthood, never to look back. Or your doctor's prognosis didn't improve, despite everyone's prayers. Or your uncle, cousin, or neighbor never admitted what he did to you, let alone said he was sorry. Or you never fully recovered from that accident. Whatever it was, it very well might not have been fair.

And unless you have faced that truth first, the pain you felt then remains real and raw and continues to dictate your emotions and actions.

In my counseling experience, I've become convinced of this simple but critical truth. It is a key to walking in victory through forgiveness. Here goes:

Pain is pain.

There is no hierarchy of pain. There are no first-place ribbons for those who got hurt the worst. Other people's issues may seem bigger than yours, or their loss may appear to be greater, but that doesn't make your pain any easier to bear. And it doesn't make forgiveness any less important. Yes, be sympathetic and even empathetic to those around you, but don't ignore your own pain.

You need not feel guilty that others have suffered more serious-sounding emotional injuries.

One of the surest ways to stop the flow of forgiveness is to compare your pain to others'. This inevitably leads you to downplay the significance of your own suffering. You may be trying to be "spiritual" by putting others first, but acknowledging and accepting your own pain leads to actual forgiveness, bringing you closer to God's heart for you.

Unforgiveness can be hidden under the trappings of a good Christian life. It may not come out in bursts of anger or a mean-spirited tongue, but it will come out—perhaps in more passive ways, such as not helping those you know you should, loving less while spending more, or even turning to alcohol or food to numb your pain.

Whatever the case, one of the first steps to forgiveness is simply recognizing that you need to forgive—acknowledging that something or someone hurt you deeply, and acknowledging that it might not have been fair.

Spend a moment with God right now, asking His Spirit to bring your heart to a place where you can do this. Maybe you need to ask Him to bring to your mind some things that you have tried to ignore but that still weigh you down. If you can, write them down. Sometimes simply writing out the offenses or what you need to forgive brings about a greater awareness that it is possible to do so.

DAY TWO

One of the greatest struggles we face on our journey of forgiveness is summed up in the tiny word "why." Why did God allow the sickness to take my child while he was still small? Why did my marriage fall apart? Why did the relationship break, the company downsize, or the bank foreclose on my home? Why did that person do that thing to me when I was that young? Why?

Only three letters, but in them we find the question that has touched each of our hearts when life just didn't seem fair.

Friend, if you can discover the answer to these three letters, you will be well on your way to finding victory through forgiveness—because you will know that there is a purpose for your pain. Freedom can be defined as a *release from illegitimate bondage, empowering you to actualize and maximize all that you were created to be*. When you are not free, you are not able to fully live out the life God has planned for you. That's why it is so important to rid yourself of the bondage of unforgiveness.

When God allows troubles and trials in your life, He has a purpose—to help you fulfill your destiny. The struggles you have faced (which may have led to unforgiveness) are not random, though they may have appeared that way. God has a purpose for what He allows.

Unfortunately, we often miss that purpose by focusing on our pain.

Through the power of forgiveness, you can dignify your difficulties by discovering the destiny God is taking you to through the mess. Just as the pain of strenuous workouts can make athletes stronger, the pain of trials and troubles can help believers grow spiritually if we don't lose faith.

In Luke 22, Jesus told Peter that Satan had asked permission to sift him like wheat. In other words, Satan wanted to mess Peter up. In this particular case, he would do it by prodding Peter to sin, which would demoralize Peter—unless he was able to forgive himself.

Satan uses a myriad of ways to mess with humanity, and one of the primary ways is through the sins we commit against each other. The sins committed against us produce in us fear, bitterness, hate, and everything that is opposite of God's greatest command and our highest purpose—to love. Fear, bitterness, and hate can lead to what I call "compounded sins." These are sins we commit as reactions, coping mechanisms, or distractions from our pain. We refuse to forgive others, making matters worse as we then feel guilty and ashamed. And then the cycle only builds.

But note that Satan had to ask permission to mess with Peter before he could do it. Even the devil is underneath God's sovereign hand. Satan can't just do whatever he wants to do. Nothing can reach you without passing through God's hand.

Yet we struggle with the question, why did God allow Satan to mess with Peter and the disciples? Why does He allow Satan to mess with any of us, for that matter? That question will frustrate you quickly if you don't live with a perspective of God's sovereignty.

God is sovereign. That means God either causes or allows everything that happens. And whether He causes it or allows it, when everything is finished, it will come out the way He wants it to come out for those who are called according to His purpose (Romans 8:28). For those who, like Peter, don't lose the faith. To lose the faith doesn't mean to lose your salvation or stop believing in God. Rather, it is a reference to giving up—choosing hate instead of love, fear instead of trust, or self-preservation instead of giving. Jesus prayed Peter would not lose the faith when Satan sifted him and tested his soul. This principle is so important that Jesus Himself prayed for Peter, and as a result, Peter held on to his faith.

Peter would be restored and lead the inaugural Christian evangelistic crusade, boldly proclaiming Jesus' name, which he had previously denied.

God's ultimate goal for you is the same as His goal for Peter—that you become a mature Christian and reflect His glory to those around you. God's method to bring you to maturity is often through trials that train. Those trials often include offenses that others have committed against you as well as the consequences of your own choices.

Why do these things happen? The ultimate answer has to do with why you have been placed here on earth, which is to live out your purpose. When you understand that God allows things to happen in order to strengthen you, you will find the courage to forgive and let go.

DAY THREE

Your view of suffering will play a large part in how easily you can forgive. If you believe all suffering should be avoided, it will be more difficult for you to forgive people who cause you pain. A biblical theology on suffering is imperative if you are to experience victory through forgiveness.

Many of us wake up each morning with burdens that seem far too great for us to bear—and the truth is, they are. However, nothing is too difficult for God. As Paul penned in one of the most well-known verses of all time, our connection with Him is the key: "I can do all things through Him who strengthens me" (Philippians 4:13).

We may never completely understand why God allows suffering, but we can know that suffering teaches us a number of things.

First, God can use suffering to draw us into a closer relationship with Him. Paul was doing God's will, yet he found himself in a Roman prison. A deep devotion to the Lord never excuses us from pain, trials, or wounds from others. However, it will draw us closer to God as we trust in His ability to strengthen and deliver us.

Second, suffering teaches us to be sensitive to those who are hurting. If we never face betrayal, pain, or loss ourselves, we will know very little about how to comfort and empathize with the people God brings into our lives—including some who have very deep needs (2 Corinthians 1:6).

Third, suffering teaches us patience and endurance—especially if we move closer to Christ through Scripture reading, meditation, and prayer. Far too often, though, instead of moving closer to Christ, we rush to find a solution. We'd rather not wait for God's will to unfold. Or worse, we seek to get back at whoever caused the suffering.

In sports, when a player is fouled and then retaliates, his reaction brings a penalty back on him. This is because he is not responsible to make judgments about infractions. Someone else is on the field to handle that—the referee or umpire. Likewise, God is positioned to respond when you are wronged. Vengeance is His, He declares (Deuteronomy 32:35; Romans 12:19). When you take your own vengeance on someone, then God—just like a referee in sports—responds to your inappropriate reaction as well as the original offense.

Suffering by the hands of others can produce bitterness, hate, and anger in some people, but it can produce grace, compassion, and love in others. It all depends on how you choose to view your suffering and whether you seek God in the midst of it, trusting in His sovereignty. Your response to suffering determines the value you receive from it.

DAY FOUR

Life feels like trigonometry sometimes, doesn't it? It gets complicated, and nothing seems to add up. But if you will start with the clear truth that God is sovereign and that He providentially arranges things to accomplish His goal, you have a lens through which to view the complexities of life that come your way and to accept them.

You and I may feel as if events occur at random, but God actually orchestrates them to serve His purposes and plans. The word "providence" means that God is sitting behind the steering wheel of history. Sometimes He's on the main highway during a bright and sunny day. Other times He's driving down dark, hidden alleys. Sometimes we might even think He's going the wrong way on a one-way street! But all the time He's steering history to arrive at His intended destination.

Because God is sovereign, He is never caught off guard. He never says, "Oops, I missed that!" What shocks you is no surprise to Him. He knew it would happen and has arranged situations and events to bring about His greater good.

In God's providence, He either has caused all things or allowed them to happen. That doesn't mean God endorses sin. God hates sin and cannot sin Himself. But even though He does not endorse sin, He will use people's sin (even when it's prompted by Satan and his minions) to accomplish His purposes.

For example, Scripture tells us that God made Pharaoh's heart hard so that God could send the plagues that would eventually lead Pharaoh to send the Jews out of Egypt. He used Pharaoh's evil intentions to teach the Israelites how to trust Him as He led them to the Promised Land. God worked with what existed within Pharaoh in order to fulfill His purpose of delivering the children of Israel out of Egypt.

God is that powerful and that good. He can use other people's harmful actions to lead you to greater freedom and life. God will never let your pain go to waste. It is wasted only when you choose unforgiveness, bitterness, and doubt rather than forgiveness, love, and trust.

In our confusion, we can easily be tempted to not

forgive. I understand. God doesn't always make sense. In fact, He rarely makes sense to our finite minds. Romans 11:33 says, "Oh, the depth of the riches both of the wisdom and knowledge of God! How unsearchable are His judgments and unfathomable His ways!"

You can't do an online search for a map or diagram that reveals God's ways. Neither can you Google or Bing "God's providence" and see the intricate details of how He does what He does and what He is planning to do in and through you.

His ways are beyond finding out. So don't be surprised when God doesn't make sense—He's not supposed to. His thoughts and His paths are higher than our own (Isaiah 55:8-9). He is the great un-figure-outable God, all the while tweaking, twisting, moving, and arranging the things that happen to you and in you to take you to where He wants you to ultimately go.

Trusting that truth is the bedrock of all forgiveness.

DAY FIVE

I wear a watch. I also carry a phone that displays the time, and I could easily pull it out of my pocket to check the time, but I still wear a watch. And I'm not the only one. Look around you—people still buy and wear watches of all different colors, styles, and sizes. Maybe you do too. Something about lifting your wrist and glancing at a watch resonates with many of us.

Some watches are fairly simple. They are digital, and the bold numbers on the screen are easy to read. Other watches are more ornate. If you were to go Switzerland, historically the watchmaking capital of the world, you would find thousands of these intricately designed watches for sale, sometimes at exorbitant prices. Yet despite how fancy or expensive they may be, all watches still basically function the same way. The person wearing the watch looks at the face of the watch to see the time.

The most interesting thing about watches is what you don't see. Hidden beneath the watch's face lies everything it needs to correctly tell you the time. The part of the watch you can see is accurate because of the parts of the watch you cannot see—all of those tiny pieces somehow connected and interrelated, all turning with one another in exactly the right order at exactly the right pace.

The same is true with God's providence and sovereignty. There is so much more going on in your life than what you can see. If you can see only the face—the surface—of the things you're experiencing, you can't understand what's really happening. Hidden beneath the events of your life are the interrelated pieces that God is weaving together to take you to your unique destiny.

When we do get a glimpse behind the scenes, we frequently misunderstand what's going on. That's why forgiveness requires trust and faith—some parts of your life just won't make sense on the surface. They may seem unrelated to one another, useless, or even damaging because you can't see the way God is using these events.

Yet God has a purpose for everything. And when you accept and trust this truth—the truth of His sovereignty over all—you will begin to see how He is using the things He has allowed in your life to get you where you need to go.

In His providence, God will bring about His intended result, and He will do it at the perfect time. Forgiveness is never based on sight. It involves your faith and not just your feelings—faith that God is moving on your behalf even in ways you cannot see or understand.

DAY SIX

If you own a dog, you probably also own a leash. The leash grants your dog a little freedom, depending on how long the leash is, so he can move about. Yet there comes a point when your dog reaches the end of his leash. When he does, the leash produces resistance that keeps your dog inside the boundaries you have set. Basically, you are controlling the distance between him and you.

I know it may not always seem like it, but the people who hurt you are on a leash. Your boss is on a leash, your neighbors are on a leash, your family members are on a leash…even Satan is on a leash. This is because a sovereign God controls how far they can go and what they can do. We see a glimpse of this in the life of Job. When Satan asked for permission to send Job through a trial, God set boundaries on how far the devil could go.

So the question might be, why does God give any room on the leash at all? Many of us might feel uncomfortable with the answer, but here it is: God sometimes uses humanity's evil to accomplish His own good.

That's probably not what you wanted to hear. We all strive for smooth sailing in our lives. We don't want problems or pain. But the greatest single statement in history on this principle reveals the most powerful truth toward freeing you to forgive, and that is Joseph's reply to his brothers who had betrayed him. He said, "As for you, you meant evil against me, but God meant it for good in order to bring about this present result, to preserve many people alive" (Genesis 50:20).

Let's focus on the word "meant" because it reveals intention. Joseph's brothers planned to harm him. They purposed to destroy him. They took pleasure in hurting him. They told Jacob, his father, that he had been killed by an animal, and in doing so, they tried to ruin Joseph's life as well as Jacob's. In other words, they thought about this. This wasn't a mistake, a slip of the tongue, or an emotional impulse. This was intentional trickery, deception, and hate.

But the evil actions that Joseph's brothers meant for bad are the same actions God meant for good. The brothers meant that mess for harm, but God meant that mess to bring Joseph into his destiny at just the right time.

Sovereignty means that God uses both the good and the bad to take us where we need to go. Life's plan includes evil and righteousness. It includes negatives and positives. Let me put it another way—God can and will use the mess other people have done to you in order to bring you to your destiny. If you will let Him, that is…if you will cooperate with Him by releasing the sins of doubt, bitterness, and unforgiveness and replace them with the virtues of forgiveness, gratitude, and faith.

DAY SEVEN

Prayers and Practicals

Dear Lord Jesus, I trust that You are working things out behind the scenes for my greater good and Your greater glory. I can't have it both ways—I can't say I trust You and then also hold on to unforgiveness. You allowed this thing to happen to me for a reason, so it would be unfair to receive the benefit of what You are doing while hating the means through which that benefit has come. Please forgive me for doubting You by hanging on to this vengeful and bitter spirit. Pour Your grace into me so I can forgive freely, and open my eyes to see beyond the surface of my life to a deeper level, where You are working all things out for good.

Prayer Needs and Requests

_____

_____

_____

_____

_____

_____

My Own Prayer

_____

_____

_____

_____

_____

_____

Practicals

1. Continue praying for God's blessing on the people you are seeking to forgive. This week, ask God to reveal to you a way to bless them even more. If you are offering unilateral forgiveness, or the person is no longer alive, you can continue to be a blessing by speaking kindly of them.

2. Make a list of the scars in your life (the negative things) that God has used for good. On the opposite side of your list of scars, write down the stars—ways that God redeemed and promoted you through this trial.

3. Keep a journal or a note open on your phone or tablet for one day and make note of each time you think or talk about the past. How much time do you spend living in the past? On the other hand, how much time and energy do you devote to seizing today and embracing a brighter tomorrow?

VALIDATIONS OF FORGIVENESS

DAY ONE

Jacob's family is one of the most dysfunctional in the whole Bible. Almost from the time of Jacob's birth, his family was in chaos. He connived with his mother to steal the family blessing from his brother. He entered a sibling rivalry with his brother that eventually threatened his life. He had 12 kids by four different women. His daughter was raped, and his sons avenged her through mass murder.

This was a family in crisis.

Perhaps you know a family plagued with chaos, dysfunction, or confusion. Maybe you grew up in one or are living in one.

But look at Genesis 35:1, where we read two very important words—"Then God." Whenever you see the word "then" in the Bible, you need to ask a question—when? In this situation, Jacob's sons had just put the family at great risk by attacking an entire city to avenge the rape of their sister. Jacob knew his household was in danger of retaliation. The family crisis had become too big to handle. The mess had no visible solution.

"Then God…"

Oftentimes, God doesn't seem to show up until things are at their worst because that's when He finally has our attention. As long as we think we can handle the situation, He waits. But when we no longer know the solution, "then God…"

God told Jacob, "Arise, go up to Bethel and live there, and make an altar there to God, who appeared to you when you fled from your brother Esau."

God had met Jacob at Bethel 20 years earlier, as we read in Genesis 28. Jacob had seen a ladder there connecting heaven and earth, with angels going up and down it.

What is your Bethel? Bethel is where God becomes real to you again. Bethel is not just reading the Bible, but sensing that God is talking to you through the Bible. Bethel is where God works out circumstances in your life and restores hope, and you wonder what you were ever so bitter about all along. Bethel is the place where God meets you intimately, heals you, and once again sets you on the path of your destiny.

God completely turned things around for Jacob. He enabled Jacob to reconcile with his brother. He restored Jacob's home. He blessed the world through Jacob's son

Joseph, who provided food during an international drought and famine.

But this deliverance depended on Joseph's willingness to forgive his brothers for serious offenses they committed against him. We touched on this briefly last week—now let's dig deeper into this epic story of forgiveness. Joseph's betrayal included elements we often see in traumatic offenses, including trickery, deceit, pain, and a disrupted life.

Joseph would wait 22 years before seeing how these offenses led to God's plan for his life, and that's a great reminder to us to be patient. We don't always see what God is doing. But Joseph kept his eyes on God through the hardships he faced—mistreatment from his brothers and from his Egyptian boss and boss's wife—so he was able to walk in victory through forgiveness.

This week we are going to consider the five validations of forgiveness, all illustrated by this one remarkable man, Joseph.

DAY TWO

Joseph's life is a tale of intrigue and suffering, treachery and faithfulness, duplicity and honesty, risk and trust…it's drama at its highest. His life has inspired movies, plays, and books. I recently finished a three-month preaching series on Joseph. His story offers so much that we can apply to our lives. Let's focus on a few things that show up primarily in Genesis 45.

This passage offers us a glimpse into one of Scripture's most pristine and comprehensive examples of authentic forgiveness. I've drawn five validations for true forgiveness from this story. Contemplate each one and apply it to your situation to determine how far you have come on your journey of forgiving those who have committed offenses against you. A memory or an event can trigger emotions you thought you had dealt with, and before you know it, you can be right back at day one, wrestling with the bitterness that has held you down all along.

The first validation is in Genesis 45:1, where we read, "Joseph could not control himself before all those who stood by him, and he cried, 'Have everyone go out from me.'" Joseph sent everyone out of the room before confronting his brothers and revealing himself to them.

You know you're serious about forgiveness when you no longer bring into the situation people who have nothing to do with the offense. Joseph didn't invite the Egyptians to stand by and watch his great act of pardon. Nor did he embarrass his brothers by putting them on display. He didn't subtly put down his brothers with biting words while exalting himself in front of his peers and coworkers. Joseph addressed his brothers' sin against him in private.

One sure way to know whether you have truly forgiven is to listen to your own lips. Do you still gossip about people who have hurt you? Do you put them down when given the chance? Are you reluctant to speak well of them when their names come up in conversations? Do you still need to vent? These actions reveal that you have not yet forgiven. You are still holding on to the pain, and it is flowing out of you in bitterness and regret.

If you need to forgive yourself, do you put yourself down when you are with other people? This is not a sign of humility but of disrespect. Or do you honor yourself by not rehearsing what happened over and over in your mind and in your conversations with others?

True forgiveness does not involve spreading the offense to people who aren't involved. (Keep in mind that this does not include a confidential counselor, pastor, or spouse.) If you intend to display the offense to others in a dishonoring way, forgiveness has not yet occurred.

DAY THREE

Here's another way to validate your progress in your journey of forgiving: Are you willing and able to put the offender at ease? "Joseph said to his brothers, 'Please come closer to me.' And they came closer" (Genesis 45:4).

Joseph called his brothers closer to him before he told them what he had to say. When you haven't forgiven someone, you want them to stay away. If you see the person walk in the same room as you, you turn to exit. If their name comes up in conversation, you change the topic or end the conversation altogether. But Joseph did just the opposite. Joseph tried to make his brothers feel comfortable in his presence, not anxious or tense or defensive.

Keep in mind that these were the same brothers who kicked him out of the family, dropped him in a pit to rot, and then decided to make some profit by selling him as a slave. Instead of judging and rejecting them, Joseph drew them near. True forgiveness creates room for repentant offenders to feel included because they have been extricated from their offenses.

How does this apply to unilateral forgiveness or to transactional forgiveness when reconciliation has not yet occurred? When people haven't repented, drawing them near is not always possible or even wise. Let their repentance stand the test of time. (More on this later.)

Do you struggle to make some people feel comfortable in your presence—even people who haven't committed offenses against you? Beware of *transference* and *representation*. Both of these principles relate to the carry-over effects of unforgiveness.

If a young woman is wounded through rape or incest,

she will often transfer that bitterness and anger to others—perhaps to men who fit a similar profile as her offender (race, age, height). This then causes distance or anger to show up in relationships with people who had nothing to do with the offense.

Or if someone stole something from you, you may apply the same level of distrust through the principle of representation to anyone with the same background or ethnicity. I can recall a time when a man borrowed thousands of dollars from me and was unable to repay me later. Each time I saw him, he gave me a reason why he couldn't pay me back.

After years of this, I knew I needed to forgive this man and release him of his debt. I did this not so much for his sake but so I could be free. I noticed a pattern emerging in my thoughts. I was filled with frustration and regret each time I saw this man (who happened to be a member of the church, so I saw him regularly), and I was also starting to distrust people in general—particularly people who wanted to borrow something from me. I was beginning to see well-intentioned friends as representatives of this man simply because they may have needed something.

If you find yourself treating innocent parties as if they had committed an offense against you and had not repented, ask God to show you the root problem—which is often a need to forgive someone else.

Don't let transference or representation ruin your other relationships.

DAY FOUR

The third way to validate where you are on the path of forgiveness is found in Genesis 45:5. Joseph told his brothers, "Do not be grieved or angry with yourselves, because you sold me here." True forgiveness helps offenders to forgive themselves when they've sought your forgiveness. Joseph could tell that his brothers regretted what they had done, especially after they had witnessed the pain they had caused their father. And so Joseph sought to help them to forgive themselves.

Joseph didn't heap guilt on top of guilt. The brothers already felt guilty for what they had done, so Joseph didn't pile more guilt on top of that.

When broken marriages come back together, and particularly if one person contributed to the breakup through addiction or an affair, verbal expressions of forgiveness and reconciliation must be followed up with consistent action. The wounded spouse must not use every new event as another opportunity to add more guilt to the offender. Don't let sarcasm or attack poison your conversations. Offer love and intimacy unconditionally rather than withholding them. If you can help offenders forgive themselves, you are gaining momentum on your journey of true forgiveness.

Joseph clearly models this third validation of forgiveness. He gives his offenders space to forgive themselves and even encourages them to do so.

This level of forgiveness can only come about when you remember God's providence. Joseph told his brothers that what they had meant for evil, God had used for good. In other words, he told them, "You may have sold me here, but God sent me here."

You must be confident that the sovereign God uses the good, the bad, and the ugly experiences in your life if you are to reach this milestone on the journey of forgiveness. Others may have messed you over, but God will use the mess to take you directly to your destiny. When you truly believe and walk in that truth, you will no longer feel the need to heap guilt on the guilty (or those you associate with the guilty by virtue of transference or representation). Rather, like Joseph, you will be motivated to use your words and actions to facilitate healing in those who have hurt you.

DAY FIVE

Today we are looking at another critical validation for forgiveness. This one shows up when we read what Joseph told his brothers to do after he expressed his forgiveness to them. "Now hurry back to my father and say to him, 'This is what your son Joseph says: God has made me lord of all Egypt. Come down to me; don't delay'" (Genesis 45:9 NIV).

Joseph wants his father to come and see that he's okay and that he is positioned for greatness—so much so that he is able to save his family from the famine. So he sends his brothers to share the good news.

We can easily miss the significance of Joseph's command to his brothers. Remember, these were the same brothers who mocked him when he shared his visions and dreams with them while he still lived at home. These were the brothers who were jealous of his gift from their father, the coat of many colors. These were the brothers who abused him and willingly tortured their dad with grief.

When we recall these things, we might expect Joseph to tell his brothers to go back to Jacob and confess everything they had done to him and to Joseph. That way, their father could get mad at them and finally give them the punishment they deserve. But instead of doing that,

Joseph protected his brothers and protected Jacob from even more hurt.

Friend, if you are holding on to the idea of vengeance—perhaps by calling it justice—you are blocking God from taking care of the situation for you. If you are trying to pay your offender back for what he or she did to you, God will step back and let you. The problem is, you aren't nearly as good at working with offenders as God is. He will perform His vengeance only when you stay out of the way.

Joseph didn't seek revenge for what his brothers had done to him. He protected them and also protected their father from hearing of the tragedy after the fact. Because of this, God was free to carry out His wrath on the brothers in whatever way He chose. For example, Judah was the leader of the group when they put Joseph in the pit. And Genesis 38 is entirely dedicated to the issues Judah and his family had to face. He lost his sons to death. His daughter-in-law tricked him into immorality and ended up having his child. His whole life seemingly crumbles around him.

Forgiving someone doesn't mean you are skipping or ignoring the justice due them. It means you are acknowledging that only God can see the heart and that He is the one who says, "Vengeance is mine, I will repay" (Hebrews 10:30). True forgiveness isn't caught up in vengeance because true forgiveness trusts God to carry it out—and to show grace and mercy.

DAY SIX

The fifth and final validation of authentic forgiveness—our last milepost to help you know where you are on this journey—might surprise you. It has nothing to do with the offense or offender, but it has everything to do with you. When you have reached this point of forgiveness in your life, like Joseph did, you will know that you have truly been released from the burden you once carried.

We find this validation in Genesis 41:50-52, where we read the names of Joseph's two Egyptian-born sons. In biblical cultures, names were chosen for their meaning and significance. That's why it's so important to note that Joseph named his first son Manasseh, which means "forget," and he named his second son Ephraim, which means "fruitfulness." Joseph was declaring that God helped him to forget his troubles and that God had made him fruitful, even in his affliction.

In essence, God gave Joseph back what the locusts had eaten (Joel 2:25) and much more. This isn't the only time we see God doing this. Consider Job's life. "The LORD blessed the latter days of Job more than his beginning" (Job 42:12). God did the same for Joseph—He made him fruitful. Remember, Joseph's family were the ones who had originally messed him over. God gave him a brand-new family, and they helped him forget the troubles in his old family. Joseph celebrated his new life of freedom from his old family and old offenses by giving his kids names that held special meaning.

Keep in mind that Joseph never forgot what had been done to him. We know this because of his words, actions, and deep feelings when he sees his brothers. However, God helped Joseph forget the pain of what had happened. He didn't forget the action, but he did forget the hurt. He was no longer living under the weight of grief, bitterness, or loss.

God also made Joseph fruitful. He blessed him in the very location of his earlier affliction.

The problem with unforgiveness is that it can keep you so locked in the past that you fail to recognize the goodness of God in the present. You can be so bound to yesterday that you miss today. In fact, that is one of the ways Satan tries to prevent you from living out your destiny. If Satan can keep you looking back, he can stop you from moving forward. But through the process of forgiveness, God helped Joseph to let go of the pain of his past and embrace a fruitful future. As a result, Joseph became successful in his home and work and eventually became a vessel through whom God blessed entire nations.

Had Joseph chosen to focus only on himself, locked in a prison of bitterness and grief, he would never have experienced the closeness with God he needed in order to interpret Pharaoh's dream, establish a plan of national productivity, and save untold thousands of people from terrible agony and death by starvation.

God has a plan for you too. And your plan has been designed to bring joy and goodness not only to you but also to others. Yet when you remain trapped under the burden of unforgiveness, you miss out on the opportunity to live out that blessing to those around you. Your willingness to forgive has to do with much more than just releasing you. It also has to do with your ability to then release and bless others through your purpose in life. Forgiveness doesn't excuse the pain. Rather, it lets it go, knowing that the pain was necessary to bring you to your purpose.

When you are able to fully forgive and thus forget the pain of the past while embracing the fruit of your present and your future, you will have arrived at the point of true forgiveness.

DAY SEVEN

Prayers and Practicals

*Dear Lord, I sometimes feel as if I have forgiven
someone, but then my actions or words reveal
that I haven't quite gotten there yet. Thank
You for being patient with me in this process
and for reminding me that it is a process. Help
me to make steps each day toward a life of
completely trusting You and letting go of the
anger and bitterness, the doubt and confusion
that sometimes plague my thoughts. Set me
free to fully enjoy the life You have created
me to live and the fruitfulness that comes
from experiencing my personal destiny.*

Prayer Needs and Requests

_____

_____

_____

_____

_____

_____

My Own Prayer

_____

_____

_____

_____

_____

_____

Practicals

1. Take a moment to thank God for each person or
   event He has allowed in your life to deepen your
   relationship with Him and grow you in spiritual
   maturity. Thank Him for using this growth
   to make you more fruitful and to bless others
   through you.

2. Choose a tangible action that will help you let go
   of the pain associated with offenses you need to
   forgive. Write them on a piece of paper, tie them
   to a helium balloon, and release them into the air.
   Or bring them to church and leave them at the
   altar in secret. Or gather some stones, associate
   each event or person with a stone, and then
   drop the stones into a lake or river. Find a way to
   symbolize your willingness to let go.

3. Give yourself grace. Be patient. Forgiveness is a process of changing your thoughts about a traumatic event or difficult person. Your decision to forgive will take time to become natural and not subject to triggers, and your emotions need even more time to catch up to your decision. Take forgiveness one step at a time. When you feel that you have failed or regressed, tell yourself, "Forgiveness is a process, and I will get there."

CONCLUSION

DAY TWENTY-NINE

Forgiving others or ourselves can be difficult. Admitting that we are having a hard time forgiving God—that can be even tougher.

Of course, this doesn't mean God has done anything wrong. We are not forgiving Him for sins He has committed, because He does not sin. In fact, just the opposite—we "forgive" Him by not attributing any wrongdoing to Him. We affirm that He is good and has our best interests in mind even when He sovereignly allows us to be wounded.

God was good even when He allowed the devil to test Job with catastrophe after catastrophe. He was good even when He told Ezekiel that He was going to take away his wife the very next day. He was good even when He gave Paul a thorn in the flesh. David, the man after God's own heart, speaks regularly about the wounds God had placed on him.

In God's sovereignty, He knows the purpose for the

pain. He sees the treasures in the trials. He understands the end from the beginning. But from our limited perspective, we often only see the wounds. And it's okay to admit—just as I'll admit—that our wounds can make us angry at God. That may not sound very spiritual, but it's best to acknowledge the truth.

The foundational principle for forgiving God, or for letting go of bitterness and anger when He allows us to experience pain, comes from Romans 8:28. In embracing the truth that all things really do work together for good when you love God and are called according to His purpose, you receive strength and wisdom to view life's trials, disappointments, and pain through the lens of God's good intentions.

When you accept that God has allowed things to happen to you because He has a greater good in store for you, you can find the freedom to respond to those who hurt you in a spirit of love. You can even seek their good. "Do not be overcome by evil, but overcome evil with good" (Romans 12:21).

To overcome evil with good, try praying for God's intervention in the heart of the person who has hurt you. Use Ephesians 1:16-23 as your prayer, substituting the person's name for the word "you." Do the same thing with Colossians 1:9-14.

Do this every day, and pray with these verses in mind.

- "This is the confidence which we have before Him, that, if we ask anything according to His will, He hears us. And if we know that He hears us in whatever we ask, we know that we have the requests which we have asked from Him" (1 John 5:14-15).

- "As the rain and the snow come down from heaven, and do not return there without watering the earth and making it bear and sprout, and furnishing seed to the sower and bread to the eater; so will My word be which goes forth from My mouth; it will not return to Me empty, without accomplishing what I desire, and without succeeding in the matter for which I sent it" (Isaiah 55:10-11).

Pray in confidence that God can change a heart and will do so in accordance with His perfect plan if you remain steadfast before Him with faith. And even if He chooses not to, your heart will be changed through this act of loving prayer for someone who has done you harm. It will soften your heart where it once was hard, enabling you to freely love and fully live out your purpose and God's plan.

DAY THIRTY

Not too long ago I went to my garage on my way to a meeting. I got in my car and pushed the garage door opener without thinking much about it.

Silence. The door stayed down.

I pushed the garage door opener again. But still nothing happened.

I got out of my car and went to the button on the wall. Pushing it over and over again, I looked at the garage door, which was now keeping me trapped in my own garage. It stayed closed, as if not wanting to be disturbed from its slumber. Glancing at my watch, I realized that if this garage door didn't open soon, I would be late. Anyone who knows me at all knows that I don't ever like to be late.

Feelings of frustration and hopelessness began to build inside me. The door was too heavy for me to lift, or I would walk over and let myself out. The garage door equipment was too complicated for me to fix, or I would fix it. So I walked over to a notice posted next to the garage door and found the installer's phone number. When I called, he asked me to check the two red lights on each side of the door.

"Are they in alignment?" he asked. I checked and quickly discovered that they were not. The small box holding the red light on the right side had been bumped, and the two lights were no longer communicating with each other.

I got down on my knees and nudged the right box back to where it belonged. Then I walked back to the button and pushed it. The garage door opened.

Friend, unforgiveness is a weight that's too heavy to lift on your own. The process of setting yourself free is often too deep and too complicated for you to figure out. Like a door that won't go up to let you out, unforgiveness traps you within yourself—until you simply get down on your knees before the One who knows you best and align your heart, thoughts, and actions with Him.

Someone else's sin may have bumped you out of alignment with God by arousing your own sins of doubt, bitterness, regret, and hate. But if you will kneel before God, confess your sins (your inappropriate reactions to what happened to you), and trust that He is sovereign and can use even the negative things in your life to take you to your perfect purpose, He will set you free. The door of doubt will rise, and you will reach your destiny.

But what about the pain? Even if I forgive, what do I do with the pain? It's still there.

Have you ever seen a bell situated high in an old church bell tower? These mammoth bells were designed to be heard for miles. Prior to today's technological advances, someone would climb the bell tower and pull a rope in order to ring the bell. Each time the bell rang, someone was holding on to the rope. That person would count how many times the bell was to ring loudly and then pull it that number of times.

Yet something would happen even when the person let go of the rope. Due to the momentum of the bell, it would continue to ring, though not as loud as before. The bell would still make a sound as it swung back and forth and back and forth.

Pain is a lot like this bell. Forgiveness occurs when you let go of the rope, but because of the momentum of your pain, it will still be there at some level. You will still feel it when you confront a trigger or a reminder of what happened. But after you have let go, you will feel it less. And as time moves on, the bell of pain will eventually subside. It will beat less forcefully on your soul and will ultimately cease altogether.

Don't be surprised when the bell continues ringing after you have chosen to forgive. Take comfort in knowing that if you have truly let go, the pain will not resound forever. It will lessen. The gaps between its triggers will grow longer. And one day, before you realize it, it will be gone.

Friend, let go of the rope. It's time to be free.

ABOUT DR. TONY EVANS

Dr. Tony Evans is founder and senior pastor of the 8500-member Oak Cliff Bible Fellowship in Dallas, founder and president of The Urban Alternative, chaplain of the NBA's Dallas Mavericks, and author of *Destiny* and *Victory in Spiritual Warfare*. His radio broadcast, *The Alternative with Dr. Tony Evans*, can be heard on more than 1000 outlets and in more than 130 countries.

THE URBAN ALTERNATIVE

Dr. Evans and The Urban Alternative (TUA) equip, empower, and unite Christians to impact *individuals, families, churches,* and *communities* to restore hope and transform lives.

We believe the core cause of the problems we face in our personal lives, homes, churches, and societies is a spiritual one. Therefore, the only way to address them is spiritually. We've tried political, social, economic, and even religious agendas. It's time for a kingdom agenda—God's visible and comprehensive rule over every area of life—because when we function as we were designed, God's divine power changes everything. It renews and restores as the life of Christ is made manifest in our own. As we align ourselves under Him, He brings about full restoration from deep within. In this atmosphere, people are revived and made whole.

As God's kingdom impacts us, it impacts others—transforming every sphere of life. When each sphere of life functions in accordance with God's Word, the outcomes are evangelism, discipleship, and community impact. As we learn how to govern ourselves under God, we transform the institutions of family, church, and society according to a biblically based kingdom perspective. Through Him, we are touching heaven and changing earth.

To achieve our goal, we use a variety of strategies, methods, and resources for reaching and equipping as many people as possible.

Broadcast Media

Hundreds of thousands of individuals experience *The Alternative with Dr. Tony Evans* through daily broadcasts on more than 1000 radio outlets in more than 130 countries. The broadcast can also be seen on several television networks and online at TonyEvans.org.

Leadership Training

Kingdom Agenda Pastors (KAP) provides a viable network for like-minded pastors who embrace the kingdom agenda philosophy. Pastors have the opportunity to go deeper with Dr. Evans as they are given biblical knowledge, practical applications, and resources to impact individuals, families, churches, and communities. KAP welcomes senior and associate pastors of all churches.

Kingdom Agenda Pastors' Summit progressively develops church leaders to meet the demands of the twenty-first century while maintaining the gospel message and the strategic position of the church. The Summit introduces intensive seminars, workshops, and resources, addressing issues affecting the community, family, leadership, organizational health, and more.

Pastors' Wives Ministry, founded by Dr. Lois Evans, provides counsel, encouragement, and spiritual resources for pastors' wives as they serve with their husbands in ministry. The ministry focuses on the KAP Summit, which offers senior pastors' wives a safe place to reflect, renew, relax, and receive training in personal development, spiritual growth, and care for their emotional and physical well-being.

Community Impact

National Church Adopt-A-School Initiative (NCAASI) prepares churches across the country to impact communities by using public schools as the primary vehicle for effecting positive social change in urban youth and families. Leaders of churches, school districts, faith-based organizations, and other nonprofit organizations are equipped with the knowledge and tools to forge partnerships and build strong social-service delivery systems. This training is based on the comprehensive church-based community impact strategy conducted by Oak Cliff Bible Fellowship. It addresses such areas as economic development, education, housing, health revitalization, family renewal, and racial reconciliation. We also assist churches in tailoring the model to meet the specific needs of their communities while simultaneously addressing the spiritual and moral frame of reference.

Resource Development

We are fostering lifelong learning partnerships with the people we serve by providing a variety of published materials. We offer booklets, Bible studies, books, CDs, and DVDs to strengthen people in their walk with God and ministry to others.

....

For more information, a catalog of Dr. Tony Evans's ministry resources, and a complimentary copy of Dr. Evans's devotional newsletter, call

(800) 800-3222

or write

The Urban Alternative
PO Box 4000
Dallas TX 75208

or visit our website:

www.TonyEvans.org

MORE GREAT HARVEST HOUSE
BOOKS BY DR. TONY EVANS

A Moment for Your Soul

In this uplifting devotional, Dr. Evans offers a daily reading for Monday through Friday and one for the weekend—all compact, powerful, and designed to reach your deepest need. Each entry includes a relevant Scripture reading for the day.

Destiny

Dr. Evans shows you the importance of finding your God-given purpose. He helps you discover and develop a custom-designed life that leads to the expansion of God's kingdom. Embracing your personal assignment from God will lead to your deepest satisfaction, God's greatest glory, and the greatest benefit to others.

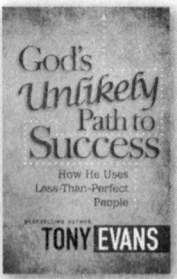

God's Unlikely Path to Success

Dr. Evans uses prominent Bible characters to show that God delights in using imperfect people who have failed, sinned, or just plain blown it. You'll be encouraged as you come to understand that God has you, too, on a path to success despite your imperfections and mistakes.

The Power of God's Names

Dr. Evans shows that it's through the names of God that the nature of God is revealed. By understanding the characteristics of God as revealed through His names, you will be better equipped to face the challenges life throws at you.

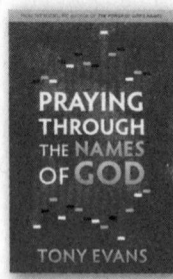

Praying Through the Names of God

Dr. Evans reveals insights into some of God's powerful names and provides prayers based on those names. Your prayer life will be revitalized as you connect your needs with the relevant characteristics of His names.

Victory in Spiritual Warfare

Dr. Evans demystifies spiritual warfare and empowers you with a life-changing truth: Every struggle faced in the physical realm has its root in the spiritual realm. With passion and practicality, Dr. Evans shows you how to live a transformed life in and through the power of Christ's victory.

30 Days to Overcoming Emotional Strongholds

Emotional strongholds come in all shapes and sizes, including doubt, rejection, and poor self-esteem. They can undermine your confidence and erode your spiritual strength. The good news is that in Christ, you can overcome these emotional strongholds. Dr. Evans shows you how to align your thoughts with the truth of God's Word and begin to enjoy true freedom.

To learn more about Harvest House books and
to read sample chapters, visit our website:

www.harvesthousepublishers.com

HARVEST HOUSE PUBLISHERS
EUGENE, OREGON